Lovers' Almanac

Lovers' Almanac

Poems by Angela Alaimo O'Donnell

Angela Alaimo O'Donnell

RESOURCE *Publications* · Eugene, Oregon

LOVERS' ALMANAC

Resource Publications
An Imprint of Wipf and Stock Publishers
199 W. 8th Ave., Suite 3
Eugene, OR 97401

www.wipfandstock.com

ISBN 13: 978–1-4982–1840-5

Manufactured in the U.S.A.   03/09/2015

For Brennan

Late, late yestreen I saw the new moon, with the old moon in her arms.

—"Ballad of Sir Patrick Spence"

*For we have seen on our way and fallen in love
with the world that will pass in a twinkling.*

—Czeslaw Milosz

*Late have I loved you
Beauty so old and so new
Late have I loved you.*

—St. Augustine

Love never fails.

—St. Paul

Contents

Acknowledgments

Grateful acknowledgment is made to the following publications in which some of these poems have appeared or are forthcoming:

Alabama Literary Review, "On Finding a Copy of *The Wellfleet Whale* in
        Wellfleet"
        "The Song of Things"

Christian Century, "On Botticelli's Annunciation"
        "For Shadowment: Villanelle for the Solstice"
        "The Hidden Life"
        "The year begins & love hides hushed"

Mezzo Cammin, "On Edward Hopper's 'A Woman in the Sun'"
        "Betrayal" (formerly, "Diagnosis: Human")
        "Anniversary Poem"
        "Homing"
        "Monosyllabics"

Post Road, "Reading Crusoe on the Metro North"

The Same, "Eurydice's Song"
        "In-somnia"
        "Wardrobe Advice"

Spiritus, "Hawk in the Bronx"

String Poet, "Un-fallen"

Valparaiso Poetry Review, "Sonnet for St. Sylvia"

Vineyards, "August 3rd & the Feast of St. Flannery"

Windhover, "Angelus"
          "Shine"

I.

Lovers' Almanac:
A Sonnet Sequence

January

Where do you want to be? she asked.
Here with you, he answered.
Here in the brusque wind
the rattle of the rafters
of our wood white house.
Here in the clutch of winter,
the month young with sun,
sparse as gleaned fields.
Here watching the cherry weep,
waiting for April to come.
Here where the lean shadows fast,
the blown birds beckon.
Where do you *want to be?* he asked.
Here with you, I reckon.

February

Here with you I reckon
I can cross the lost world
and still keep my self, she said.
Her mother had been dead
two years the first day
of the Heart Month,
her birth month
now become her dearth month.
It never goes away,
she said and sighed—
then turned back to earth
and his bright face
as if all her worth
lay in his embrace.

March

She lay in his embrace
and he in hers
when the world broke in.
The ground woke again
thrust new shoots into outer air.
She rose, washed her hair,
and both became young again.
They walked the river walk
as king and queen.
She missed the other shore,
the place she'd lived before,
though in her dreams
she ran the lake again
and owned it once more,
the sky always bluer than it seems.

April

The sky never bluer than it seems
in easy spring,
Easter white and bird-egg blue.
My gift is me to you,
she said the date she'd
been born. *What's yours to me?*
she smiled. The cherry wept
blooms in the yard. He kept
her gift in a box of thought.
Not a thing that could be bought—
a year without a fight,
dinner every night,
each day a new start,
a wild heart.

May

A wild heart rules the month of May,
the boy-girl, maypole-dancing days,
the ancient pulse of germ and birth,
in the ground and in the blood.
Leave the safety of the hearth,
drown your dry life in the flood.
Farewell breath of autumn's being.
Welcome sweetly earth's new greening.

Now let's sex beneath the trees,
cross my heart and spread my knees.
Faith, to you, I give my all.
They hear the cardinals' common call,
steady pair that weds for life,
he claims his color and his wife.

June

He claims his color & his wife,
red for mirth & red for song.
They sing their tune & love their life
and live together long.
And so our marriage, for the birds,
must seem to mimic their good match.
We suffer from the same old urge
to brood our eggs & watch them hatch.

Our young have come & gone, my love
and now we keep our quiet hours,
except when they return and move
our minds back to their youth and ours.
We loved the clamor and confusion
and savored Spring's sweet delusion.

July

Why savor Spring's delusion
here in the heat of summer?
deny July's intrusion
though he be a late comer?

The feast we've spread upon the grass
as green as earth can ever be.
Let's break our daily fast
as evening falls beneath the trees

where you and I have stretched our souls,
the length of oaks, our easy limbs
touching knees & breasts & toes,
happy in our venal sins.

An old-school couple couples here.
How like you this, she asks, *my dear?*

August

How like you this, she asks, *my dear?*
Though his pleasure is quite clear
as August steals July's desire
and sets the month of fire on fire.

Sunrise late and sunset long
now so far beyond the solstice
brings its end-of-season song,
sea and sand late summer's solace.

They climb the dunes and watch the stars
come out each lunar evening.
He looks for Venus, she for Mars.
They hear the ocean keening.
The ghost crabs flit across the beach.
The moon floats just beyond their reach.

September

The moon floats just beyond their reach
as fall sounds its early call.
The slant light arrives to preach,
again, the loss of all.

They watch another autumn come,
chill their nights & warm their days,
steal their hours, one by one,
till summer's swept away.

They light a fire upon the hearth
that has been cold these easy months.
Another season's left its mark,
performed its acrobatic stunts.
Nothing lasts but us, she said.
We'll never be among the dead.

October

We'll never be The Dead, she said
amid the month of Halloween,
as if to dare the spirits there
who walk unheard and walk unseen.

She knew she'd spoke a heresy.
He knew she'd told a lie.
(Yet what a tender mercy
to think your love might never die.)

Surely they were not the first
to hope they'd live forever.
All lovers know the curse
that falls on all—but never

believe it will divide *this* pair.
They feed their faith, deny despair.

November

They feed their faith, deny despair,
embrace the season of the Saints,
read their favorites (Francis, Clare)
who loved the world with no restraint.

They've done with less and do with more
the season of the sealed door,
the windows shut against the cold,
their hearts refusing to grow old.

The geese that gather travel south,
the clouds collect and threaten snow,
while these two love from hand to mouth
and have no place they long to go.

Here is where they've taken root.
No other life would suit.

December

No other life would suit this pair.
They feed their faith, deny despair:
They'll never be among the dead.
The moon floats just beyond their reach.
How like you this, my dear? she says,
as spring's sweet song still sings to each.
This steady pair that weds for life,
two hearts wild as a month of Mays,
the sky true as a tuneful wife
whose husband lives in her embrace.
Again they watch the cherry weep.
The summer soon will beckon.
Where do you want to be?
he asks. *Here with you, I reckon.*

II.

Homing

Baltimore Harbor

The places where you put in time
        become homes you must return to.
The way bits of yourself stud
        the pink brick, the white drift of sky.
The way the wave of the place traces
        the curve of your young spine.
The way it winds itself around
        the lashings of your rocky heart.

And still you return, like gulls that cry
        and lap the harbor, announcing the spot.
Here to define the horizon of your life,
        sweet arena of your stump and stage.
Church spire, ship's mast, Key Bridge, smokestack.
        How it wounds you each time you come back.

Angelus

Always the rumor of music,
the hollow longing of the bell
rung by noon and evening light
the harrowed hymn of praise.

Always the beating of wings,
majestic messenger on fire,
her virgin words a calm catastrophe,
the end of ordinary time.

Always my mother's echo
out the back porch door,
our game called to a halt,
the ball left in the darkening yard.

Always singing me home.
The only poem I own.

On Botticelli's Annunciation

I have met them in the Uffizi,
the angel hunched on bended knee—
his thigh thick beneath his satin robe—
the virgin's urgent *contrapposto*,
her sudden arm extended long
beyond the border of her cape
halting his rehearsed song
as if his theme weren't love but rape.

Her face impossibly serene
does not betray her body's fear.
His deathless eyes have never seen
a mortal woman quite so near.
The space between their outstretched hands
salvation in a single glance.

Pas de Deux: The Lovers

Alvin Ailey Dance Performance
February 14th

They move against the smooth reserve of art,
the space dividing heart from eager heart.

Her taut body, goaded by desire,
slides in slow obedience to fire,

metal to magnet, flesh of soft steel,
an empty vessel urgent to be full.

Two lovers pool in sweet solution.
One begins the pull of separation.

Her eye declines. She will not be possessed.
His arms that had so tenderly caressed

close now in straight embrace, so devoted
only a saint would feign not to notice

how difficult it is to breathe and to hope,
how absolute the hand upon her throat.

Eurydice's Song

And part of you leaves Tartarus
But part stays there to dwell—
You who are both Orpheus
And She he left in Hell."

—A.E. Stallings, "Song for the Women Poets"

Another woman having it all
life as both singer and sung to,
hearing the lover's siren call
yours the arms you would run to.

Being the sought and the seeker,
leading your life upon life,
tasting of oil and vinegar,
being the bread and the knife.

This the trick of your art,
how to be maker and made,
knowing the end from the start,
playing until you get played,

loving the touch of your own skin,
no wonder you invented him.

Wardrobe Advice

"O wear your tribulation like a rose."
—W.H. Auden

Thumb the gentle stem. Careful of the thorns.
Touch its velvet petals to your wrist.
Sniff its stiff scent with courage. Do not mourn
the idle easy blooms you might have picked.
Clutch it close. Don't hold it at a distance.
A rose's place is nearest to your heart.
Learn to love your new need for persistence.
Keeping it alive your (un)chosen art.

Wear it on your brow like a warrior.
Wear it on your thigh like a whore.
Bear it in your hand like a courier.
Grip it in your teeth. Fling it to the floor.
Crush it with your sole, your healed despair.
Pick it up. Place it in your hair.

On Edward Hopper's
"A Woman in the Sun"

She steps into the length of light,
a woman clothed with the sun.

A cold comfort this lemon dawn,
her shadow vestige of the night.

Thin-ribbed, full-fleshed, she fronts the day
as if some truth were offered new

besides the cogent call of blue,
besides reprieve from twilight's gray.

Nothing can be mistaken here
where summer's clarity is kind.

Her body's urgency so clear
against the darkness of her mind.

What she sees we'll never know.
She stands so naked and so clothed.

Betrayal

The star of my left breast
    bloomed on the blank screen,
her many ducts like finger lakes—
    so full she seemed.

Ever the lesser breast,
    always short on milk,
never well-equipped,
    not her bigger sister's ilk.

Now she was special,
    her little lump new.
Still, she looked to me
    harmless and true.

You could have felled me with a feather—
    I was that struck—
as she stood there in the mirror
    dumb as luck.

III.

Sunrise in Sicily

Etna's smoking and the sky's on fire,
province of the lord of light.
First fierce color, then sweet heat,
the ready rise of blinding white.
What beauty rules the westing day?
What future bodes so broad and blue?
Thick night thins and wisps away
and lends these hours to me and you.

So, love, what shall we do with it—
the pearl that's placed in our own hands
plucked from some dark oyster bed,
palmed miracle of sea and sand.
The round perfection of the thing
enough to make the sun god sing.

Mindfulness

"Our minds are like crows. They pick up everything that glitters."
—Thomas Merton

She flits like the dark bird she is
darting from treetop to hedge,
strutting the stone window ledge,
stalking the light's bright pieces.
The sliver of tin in the tall grass,
the penny under the overpass,
the shiny shard of broken glass
are treasures to her species.

She gathers every bit of life
her narrow beak can hold,
her cluttered nest rife
with gaud that gleams like gold.
Each flitting brings another find.
She claims it hers and makes it mine.

Monosyllabics

"One day she fell in love with its heft and speed."
—Josephine Jacobsen, "The Monosyllable"

I.

Day two
she sees
what more
it can do:

Speak *he* & *she*,
thou & *thee*,
me & *you*—

Teach school,
bird & *word*,
beast & *feast*,
sage & *fool*—

Hold the world
in small
(its rise & fall)—

Count one to six, eight to ten—
Thick & thin friend,
Love the lone & the odd—
Name God.

II.

Day three,
part & whole,
flesh & soul,
sing their tune:

hip & *lip*,
thigh & *eye*,
heart & *art*.

Time & tomb,
spell out doom.
Scourge & cross
seals the loss.

Flesh & bread
serve as sign,
and this blood
once was wine.

The Word holds
Child of God
yet not
di-vine.

III.

Day four:
the small hours,
days & weeks,
months & years,

all pool here
in the tin cup
of time—

but not
the wild loves
of a night heart,

not
the brief breaths
of the day's part

where we live
and die
most true.

Try to paint
the green world
with no blue.

On Finding a Copy of
The Wellfleet Whale in Wellfleet

I hefted you in my hands,
        sturdy friend,
                traced the woven ropes
stretched across your boards,
        the black ink print
                three-inch square—
blue window to the sea—
        the curling waves,
                the grounded ships,
the great dead beast borne ashore.

I loved your narrow sorrow
        the lore of the local
                announcing abroad,
What happened here
        matters & how,
                your strange tale

pulling me out (and in),
        helpless fish hung
                at the end of each
cunning and undulant line.

Like him
        you seemed to ask of us
                not sympathy, or love,
or understanding,
        but awe and wonder.

I pressed you, a promise
        against my breast,
                carried you down the cloister walk
of the dusty book shop,
        then set you down
                on the counter
a place and a state

as something to come back to,
        a wild prize
                not proper to be caught

until I saw the hand,
        your poet's mark,
                blue news inked across the page,
the *Master of the whale-roads*
        already gone the way
                of his own Wellfleet Whale—
you his song,
        his signature and sign,
                disgraced and mortal
                        and mine.

August 3rd & the Feast of St. Flannery

dawns and yawns
across the horizontal world,
the one she cleaves
with hawk's eye, she,
the wife of the countryside,
probing crack
and wretched crevice,
tracing the weft of suffering
that nets us all—

the men in their toast-colored hats,
the women with bad hearts
& ice-picks for eyes,
the tattooed loser loving
the Lord in his mortal skin,
the whore heavy as a forklift,
tractors benignly firing the sky,
homicidal bulls and their brutal kin—

each piercing the dark heart
as armless they gesture,
legless they stand
up to be counted and mean,
not one of us lost or lonely,
but each deeply adored,
their maker fond
of her children as any

nit-picking monkey
in a Chinaberry tree

or country-wise fool who knows
grace when she smells it,
fresh as pines swaying drunk
in the rivering rain,
sure as the poplar raising
all its palms in the air,
each leaf inked with praise,
each pattering prayer.

The Hidden Life

There are many other things that Jesus did,
but if these were to be described individually,
the whole world could not contain the books that would be written.

—John 21:24-25

He cried when he slid out, a slippery fish,
his mortal lungs unready for the rush.
He took his mother's breast like a starved kid.
He craved meat young, forced his fist in the dish.
He tottered to his feet when he was one,
and brought his father to his eager knees.
He learned to walk, but never learned to run.
He napped, read books, talked to the trees.
When he turned twelve, he fell in love with fire.
He'd light his torches underneath the stars,
heave them towards the lights in the night sky
mapping the distance, counting the hours.
He studied the sun as it rose and fell.
He envied it, but did not tell.

Shine

You are the light of the world, he said
and meant it. He conjured them to shine.
His voice that clear. His words that fine.
A few months later he'd be dead.

But even so, they still would shine.
Not under baskets, like he said.
No holding out. No playing dead.
They took big risks and paid the fine.

Give light to all the house, he said
and meant it. Then he'd shine.
They thought that all would work out fine.
They didn't know they'd end up dead
as we all do, come rain or shine.
Even as the lights went out, they felt fine.

A Cana Blessing

for Charles & Elise
June 29, 2013

When Christ came to Cana he changed the game.
There could not be a wedding without wine.
The water that he stirred could not remain the same.
The wine as it aged would get better with time.

And so Christ comes to touch these lovers here,
to change young love into love full and fine,
love that pours out plenty from year to year.
love in such excess it is theirs and yours and mine.

This is their miracle. Now love comes to call
and knocks on every heart in this room.
As these lovers pledge nothing less than all
from this day through the dawn of doom,

let us bear witness, raise our glasses up,
to so much love spilling out the cup.

IV.

Safe Passage

Rocked all night in the sea's dark arms
we tended toward that distant shore
skimming the surface of our sleep
expecting more

than any life can rightly give—
the magnitude of sunlit days
we had already loved and lived
shrouded in a haze.

Now beneath a star-pocked sky
our freighted ship plows heavy seas.
The bone-cold fact that we will die
freezes me.

Your warm body next to mine
eases me.

Unfallen

"I was happy, happy, happy, happy, happy!"
Philippe Petit upon completing his high-wire walk
between the Twin Towers, August 4th, 1974

The day he tossed his line across
        and tricked heaven
was not a day like all his other days.
        Walking tight along the wire
he kissed the world's abyss,
        charmed the wind into thinking
he had wings he could ride
        if his ordinary legs should fail.
He asked the sun to hide its eye
        so the eyes in the canyon looking
up could see *him* against the sky.

So a young god eclipsed
        an old for an hour,
less than a sixth
        of one day's rise.
No one would remember
        the weather that day.
All they would recall is the fall
        the small man dared and delayed,
how the towers swayed,
        and after his mad dance
how still they stayed.

Reading Crusoe on
the Metro North

or, at least, a version of him,
the one Miss Bishop (over)heard
lamenting England's dull clime,
the lack of color and the smack
of life he'd learned to love
on his first island.

Manhattan slides by, another island,
though unlike either of his—
the rivers that slice land from land
slender, civil, navigable,
crossed by daily train
to the solid Bronx.

Traveling together, we are all
alone, wholly rapt
in our *Times* or Kindle,
iPhones humming in our lax hands,
friends sending word across
earth and air,
refusing to desert us.

If Crusoe could, he'd call his man
who kept him sane and taught him love.
But city sickens the free soul
and good Friday proved no match
having lived so long in solitude,
leaving Crusoe more alone

than he'd been after the first wreck,
himself become one more island.

My phone is full of ghosts.
I do not erase them.
It is my wild hope
that it will one day ring
and the name of my dead
will flash across the screen,
cross over the divide
that slices land from land,
sure as this train
on which I and Crusoe ride.

Hawk in the Bronx

"My heart in hiding stirred for a bird."
—Gerard Manley Hopkins

Perched on a church
scolding stone

Hawkeye owns
his daily glory.

He wives the wind
and chides the world

whose children make
their earthward way

asleep beneath the wing
of their unknowing.

Being pure bird,
minor miracle of air,

he is stranger to despair,
the ordinary agony

that halves the merely
human heart.

The easy feast he devours
each of every bell-knelled hour

escapes those who live too low.
Twice-blessed is he to know

the saint's sweet rapture
impossible to capture.

The Song of Things

"Making use of the useless—a beauty we have less than not deserved."
—Wendell Berry

The feather shed (its bird fled)
dropped on an old stone
dislodged from the wall (hence its fall)
calls its owner home.

The bottle cap, the fabric scrap,
portions good and small,
ghost their missing counterparts
each adumbrating all.

Nail clippings, lipstick tubes,
pens empty of their ink,
the chipped coffee mug
in the brown-stained sink.

The heart loves the left and the lame.
No two beauties are ever the same.

Putting My Sons on My C.V.

where they belong
as sure as all those poems,
attempts and essays
to carve the clean bone,

all the while
tending to their tender flesh,
kissing limbs, rocking bodies
against swollen breasts,

blood-hungry, loving my own
all day and all night,
swearing my true home
was the library's white

walls, the classroom's hollow
halls, where the sons of others
came to hear my thoughts
on the poems of not-mothers.

What did I know of art
but the urgent hunt of love,
the desperate *do, do, do*
of the halfway heart

full only in the company
of what I'd made,
the lines of music I'd laid
in each infant tongue?

I no more pretend
this is separate from me,
this mother-love-without-end
that has altered me

subtle as tsunami,
easy as earthquake,
cuddly as a corpse,
deniable as destiny.

All my history is blood and words,
each poem I've heard,
Three Sons my best song.
My C.V. isn't long.

Late Love Poem

What if I wanted to begin again,
the small down of an infant's skin
exactly what you hoped for in the nick
of this particular time, O love of mine?

What if I gathered all the flesh I'd lost
and gained along my limbs these thirty years,
molded me into my sixteen-year-old
self, hungry for our life, careless of the cost?

What if you said *Sure! Why not?* and *When
are we gonna get married?* asking *where?*
and not *would you?* or *whether*, so sure
were you of me and I of you, my dear?

And what if you say *Yes* and I say *Yes?*
And what if you say *How?* as I say *Now?*
I'd laugh loud as Sarah, chant Weird Sisters' charms,
fold my old man into these young-again arms.

September's Song

Slant says September, and *easy rain*,
the days dropping fast as chestnut leaves.
The long promises of May's brief reign
teach us that summer ever deceives.

Nothing goes gentle into winter's night.
The ivy clamors, never more alive.
Birds announce the worm and take fresh flight.
The bees refuse retirement to their hive.

All dissolves in the certainty of fall.
Tell the geese who sound their rebel call.
Tell the cricket, who sings her lucky song.
Love, says September, *it won't last long.*

V.

For Shadowment:
Villanelle for the Solstice

Here, here in the crook of the year,
the crux and fix and flux of the year
light falls long across and dear.

Here in the ruck and dreck of the year
We glean and gather grace and gear,
here, here in the crook of the year.

Here is the neckbone of the year,
its knuckle sharp, its blade sheer,
where light falls long across and dear.

Hear the matins of the year,
the chant of praise and marrow fear,
here, here in the crook of the year.

Cheer the vespers of the year,
the prayers that rise from tongue to ear
as light falls long across and dear.

Clear your mind as night draws near.
Stead your heart and shed no tear.
Here, here in the crook of the year
where light falls long across and dear.

Dreaming of Emily Dickinson

I woke last night to Emily,
an envelope in hand,
in all her scrupulosity
divining its demands.

She worded every cornice
with ink and ready pen,
her heart a roaring furnace,
her gaze a firmament.

The envelope stayed steady
upon her writing desk.
The poet moved around it
as she bowed and confessed

the thoughts that still a wild mind
that rock an empty house,
and when she folded it again
she thumbed her seal and sign.

The envelope remained unsent.
The snow piled up outside.
Summer came and summer went.
And Emily died.

Sonnet for Saint Sylvia

February 11th, 4:30AM

Now's the very time that she did it.
Time both of day and of year.
The violet hour, between wake and sleep.
Her milk-fed boy in the sealed room.
The poems stacked neat. The kitchen clean.
Her wifely duties quite done.

Only then did she kneel at the oven.
Her heart untrained for distance.
Tired of the hurdling, tired of the run.
Dying to rest before morning
cracked the door on another gray day.
She sought the darkest places she knew—
the basement, the oven, the grave.
There she could be brave.

In-somnia

I wake alone in the curve of the dark
       marooned on an island of sound,
hissing radiators, passing cars,
       the howl of a single hound.

We, the people, the Republic of Watch,
       tourists in the precincts of sleep,
weight the floorboards, fill empty rooms,
       listen to our loves breath deep.

Mind and flesh make a mismatched pair,
       each a creature of desire—
one seeks stillness, the other urge,
       rhyme of shadow and fire.

Bound for life, we make our somber round,
       longing to get up, longing to lie down.

Elegy for Benjamin

"Think of me, forget me not, remember me wherever you go."
—African Folk Song

Some of the light leaves the world today.
Snow drops low from the heavy sky,
lays down soft on the ground's green gray.

You were the boy who loved words, the play
of sound and sense that fired your eye.
Some of that light leaves the world today.

You sang like a saint, took us all the way
to heaven without our having to die,
no need to lie down on the ground's green gray.

You showed us that joy was a means to pray,
your bright smile ghosted your soul, wise and shy.
Some of your light leaves the world today.

You knew in your bones you'd leave us one day,
such darkness of mind makes us grieve and sigh
as we lay you down on the ground's green gray.

Our hearts refuse to say goodbye.
Forget me not, you sign and say.
Some of the light left the world today
and you lie deep in the ground's green gray.

Anniversary Poem

February 1, 2013

Three years gone and each return
I feel you far from me.
Lying flat in your boat
you drift and float
beyond where eye can see.

When will I ever learn
keeping you company
in my childish heart
with my childish art
won't bring you back to me?

The seasons tack and turn.
The snow beats and the sun burns.
And I, your reckless daughter,
watch you, who feared all water,
sail bravely out to sea.

On Leaving the Inferno

"And we walked out once more beneath the stars."
—Dante, final lines of The Inferno

After the wandering in the wood,
After the carnal chasing flesh,
After the wrathful thumping the sullen
After the hell of endless death—
After the fraudulent and violent,
After the river made of blood,
After the agon of the suicides,
After the lustful without love—

After the panderers & flatterers,
The hypocrites & thieves,
The liars & the traitors,
The dead men turned to trees—

They bore the dark inside of them
back to the world of light again.

The year begins &
love hides hushed

in the brambles and in the brush,
in the long shadows on the long street,
in the creases of the faces that I greet.
Dryad of my back yard,
Apollo of my morning,
bell tones hefted heavenward,
musk of hardwood burning,
my wild hand that guides the pen,
my tame heart that wilds when
all cries *love!* and *love!* again.
O beauty, O fast friend,
your touch upon my parchment skin,
youngs it new. The year begins.